RISE LIKE A PHOENIX FROM YOUR ASHES

Transform your life through the power of habit change and self-awareness

BY

SARA NUR

DEDICATION

I wanted to prove myself wrong by writing this book. Anything is possible. Just set your mind to it and believe in yourself.

And, to my better self as I remind myself first, before I remind you, of my civil duty as we explore the wondrous journey we experience, called Life.

Table Of Contents

INTRODUCTION

WHY ARE YOU HERE?

Hello friend, it is quite the pleasure to meet you. Before we begin, I would like to take a moment to thank you for considering me and my God-given ability to help you change your life and the world. Most importantly, I want to thank you for investing in YOU and showing up for YOU. I believe we are our best advocate and we must show up for ourselves. So, congratulations on saying yes to yourself and taking a step forward to improve your life and begin to break the habits that have been withholding your growth. The hardest part is finding the courage and strength to follow-through in showing up, but here you are. Here you are not for me, but for you and your self-empowered betterment. This is your journey and I am here to help you along the way. We will be spending some quality time together while I help you turn your unmotivated- and unsuccessful-feeling life all the way around. Instead, you will be experiencing simple changes that will help enrich and fulfill your life, allow you to let go, and position yourself where you want to be in this life and the afterlife. All through the power of choice.

Showing up is one component, but *how* you show up is the important additional piece to the puzzle. The way to measure this is by looking at the alignment of your thoughts and actions, and how you choose to show up. Let me ask you this. Are you ready to show up? If the answer is yes, how do you choose to show up? How do you want the world to see you? Over the years, copious people have confessed that I am gifted with a contagious and abundant supply of motivation and energy, passion and ideas. Of course, I am a go-getter and not afraid to try new things within reasonable and practical limits. I am an activator, achiever and courageous enough to initiate things or conversations that are of importance to me. I remember my friends, colleagues, bosses, classmates, and even strangers, have told me that I have this unspoken potential and the ability to make something happen out of my life. It is all about the way you choose to show up and carry yourself and how others perceive you.

I still remember vividly that every year during parent-teacher conferences at school, my teachers would continually say, "Don't forget about me when you become famous and successful." I have my entire educational history laminated in a large binder, so, in case you are wondering, I have got the proof. You would have to be a brick to not feel instant motivation from praise and encouragement like that, seriously! But being young and going through my childhood years with innocence and a certain degree of aloofness, I did not quite grasp the concept of the feedback I was receiving. I wish I remembered the moment it clicked, but I do not think it was just one moment where it clicked. My soul tells me it was a series of small and large events of varying significance that opened up the wisdom for me to understand. It took me a while to believe in myself and truly open my eyes to the mere potential of what could be for me. Now that I know, yes, I have a lifetime of work to do, but, I also have a strong sense of never ending hope.

In the past, a perpetual pattern I noticed I was implementing was thinking I either achieved something or not, and it was as black and white as that. Afterall, Albert Einstein once said, "Creativity is intelligence having fun." I am intelligent and I am creative; having both to lean into are wonderful resources towards the journey of growth. I do believe it has a lot to do with my upbringing, being a third-culture kid, being multilingual, and growing up in a way that was very unique, to say the very least. I am still wrapping my head around my identity and experiences thus far. In the past, I did not wholeheartedly believe in myself and never understood why I could not see past the black and white. Remember what Einstein said about creativity being intelligence having fun? The gray area is just as good because it allows for self-exploration and the discovery of a sense of self. Self-belief was part of my discovery and journey to closeness to Allah (God), higher wisdom, accountability, purpose, clarity, connectedness, empathy, intentional communication, forgiveness, letting go, and interpersonal interactions that enrich the soul and provide peace and harmony.

Having potential and surpassing it is a creatively gray area experience that we face throughout our entire lives. It is a matter of taking what you know, enriching your skills with new ones, and taking potential to mastery. There will be challenging moments in life where you will face deciding if you have what it takes or not, but either choice means you are in tune with yourself. That this opportunity may or may not be for you, but you know your best self to answer that honestly. Or at least, you should know your best self. It is not the end of the world, although it may seem like its walls are closing in on you.

Take a deep breath.
Take another one.
This is why you are here.

Life is about understanding our purpose with our God-given talents, but it has to do with our character and how we take our lessons, experiences, or aha moments to the next level of greatness. It is about our willingness to learn, grow, and improve ourselves while learning to enhance the way we show up. By learning, we are in turn able to teach others who are open and willing to learn. That is what life is about - giving and taking. There is no need to live a life that is dull and passive. The quality of life is what people pursue, but it can be on a superficial and materialistic level that is unfulfilling. Let us nourish our souls by chasing the active life and freeing ourselves from the toxic, passive one.

The purpose of this book is to serve as a guideline to help those in need build a strong foundation where you will make small changes without even knowing you are making them. Small hinges swing big doors. The small, consistent changes you make and commit to will open up your life in ways you never imagined. I want to provide you with a guide on how you can find motivation within yourself and radiate it outwards to reflect upon your life. This is to help you make tangible what you have been unsuccessfully trying to bring to fruition. It is time to quit making excuses and make it happen. It is time to take action. I want to make my mark on this earth before I leave it, and it should be everyone's goal to do the same, at least in one way. If I can help even one person, I have accomplished one of my purposes in life. Join me while we embark on this self-discovery journey. Let's get it!

Xoxo,
Humble Muslim human being, first
Abundance and Transformational Coach, second
Sara

CHAPTER 1

BELIEF IN GOD

We sometimes are engrossed in the mundane, routine aspects of our lives to the extent that we forget what truly matters. It is human nature to be focused on what the heart desires, even though it lacks substance. Priorities are skewed or entirely disregarded, but this is the current lens through which we see the world in front of us. But, for the world in front of us to exist, the divine world must also exist. Religion and the belief in God are crucial and the foundation of living. Your connectedness with God and the remembrance of Him is the main ingredient in producing a platter of life with a certain quality level.

Faith is crucial in a person's life, and in my case, it is a way of life. I am a Muslim woman, and I believe in Allah being the only deity, his prophets, Messenger Muhammad (Peace and Blessings be Upon Him). I believe that there exists a Heaven and a Hell, there will be a Day of Judgement, and that everyone is born into this world innocent. I believe that every being has their destiny pre-written by Allah, and we have the gift of free will, the ability to choose, which can alter what was pre-written. I believe, through a lot of prayers and a direct connection to Allah, that your heart's deepest conflictions and your uneasy soul will be soothed and put at ease. My belief in Allah has never wavered, but I have noticed a fluctuation in my level of faith throughout my life. This means that I must continue to believe and, in turn, strengthen my soul in an almost flowing and ebbing way. Such moments of self-awareness lead to improvement because you then comprehend the importance of doing so and the ensuing fulfillment. We are human and are not created to be perfect. We need not fall into the trap of using this fact as a scapegoat when we fall short.

I can recount various periods in my life where I lost belief in my value, skill set, and self. I began to feel overwhelmed and experience the effects of unknown anxiety issues creeping up on me. In the past, I have responded to this sort of feeling by procrastinating, asking for new deadlines to procrastinate, being lazy, doing other things to deflect from the task at hand, bingewatching TV, or sleeping. I would do anything possible to avoid accomplishments, spiraling into this abyss of sadness and depression. I found myself suddenly crying in my cubicle, not being able to pinpoint the true nature of my distress. A heavy feeling followed in my heart that would disallow me to sleep. I would not focus and was constantly miserable, despite my visage wearing a facade that I had mastered. The lack of sleep would make me sleep my entire weekend away, and the cycle continued for months. I let this go on for too long until I realized I had more

control than I believed I had. I awoke to the fact that I needed to hastily make a change and pray to Allah to give me strength, focus, and determination to achieve my goals.

There is a supplication that I keep close to me from a top-rated and standard Muslim prayer book called Hisnul Muslim (Fortress of the Muslim), written by Sa'id bin Ali bin Wahf Al-Qahtani. This is the go-to prayer guide for literally every situation, with duas (supplications or prayers) from the Quran and the Prophet Muhammad (SAW). Though this book may be pocket-sized, do not be fooled by the power of Allah's word. This book contains a supplication that protects against grief, incapacity, laziness, cowardice, debt, miserliness and being overpowered. I had hit the jackpot, and the healing I experienced on a soul level was a sign of staying on this track. With Allah's guidance and allowance, I have been able to suppress feelings of defeat. Belief in Allah is one of the tools that I have found very useful in finding purpose in life. We have to remember Allah all the time, in good and evil, for Him to remember us.

In the grand scheme of things, it is our responsibility and duty to understand what is right and wrong and how that applies to our daily life. We must take accountability for what we do and say. It is challenging and highly uncomfortable at times, but it is essential. Having a solid belief in God keeps us in line with the higher power, our creator. It is a humbling feeling to remember that there is something bigger than me. It is also reassuring to know that when I feel lost or that my moral compass has no distinct direction, I seek solace in that Allah is looking out for me. He is protecting me and guiding me on the right path, so long as I choose to put in my work and do good along the way. The key to this is maintaining your belief in and connectedness to Allah. When you feel completely lost and pray for His guidance, He will always direct you to what is best for you. If you do not pray for His guidance, most times, you will find yourself getting farther and farther away from the right path and away from success. The facade of this world misdirects us from the reality of the afterlife, and our actions with the right intention will determine our success in entering the gates of jannah (heaven).

Are our actions and decisions in alignment with what our moral compass tells us? Are we hypocritical by telling people one thing and personifying another? If you believe in God, are you thanking and praising Him for all the blessings you have received? Some do not believe in God, and some believe in a higher power. Approaching it with curiosity, maybe they have not yet found that connection with the Almighty, and perhaps that is why they might notice something inside is missing.

I believe that every sane person should approach life and the decisions made with a basic moral compass, at the very least. That inner conscience we each have is our soul guiding us through life. We must heed what it tells us because this is the source of anything related to self. Intuition and connectedness to oneself are natural, and it is vital to listen to that internal you. It can be frightful how accurately our intuition can guide us into and out of certain situations, whether the awareness is shortterm or long-term. I cannot articulate enough how success comes from doing good in the world, praying, asking for forgiveness, and giving charity. If your morals, ethics, or values are compromised, your soul will tell you. If you are feeling lost, do not stop believing in God and seeking His guidance. There is a suitable place and time for everything as everything is prewritten. The next time your intuition goes off, stop for a moment to evaluate the moment with curiosity. You will make a better-informed decision, and the outcomes will be more fruitful to you and those around you.

CHAPTER 2

---◆---

ACKNOWLEDGE, RECOGNIZE, ACT

At some point in our lives, we may question the circumstances of difficulty that come our way, but somehow, we find a way to adapt to and cope with these struggles. We have to remember that gratitude is one of the keys to ease in this life. I have become better at exercising gratitude, and I am very grateful for my blessings thus far. Being alive and able to breathe every day is a huge blessing in itself, but we get so caught up that we tend to forget this. On the same token, however, I cannot help but feel conflicted because I know that I have not reached my most tremendous potential.

My heart tells me I have yet to make myself and my mom proud because I do not feel my capabilities have come to fruition. I have not yet fulfilled my destiny and purpose, creating this appetite for more and thoughts of what I need to do to get there? This drives me into taking some action and initiating the execution of some plans. What is my purpose here? I have no clue, but I am on a quest to find out. It is human nature to respond by focusing on the destination and its enrichment when we absorb the lessons and wisdom gifted to us by the journey itself. It is not the outcome, rather your openness to the process, that will prepare you for the realities of life and make you a better person. However, it all depends on your decisions and the choices you make when faced with specific situations.

I try to acknowledge and recognize that no matter what roadblocks I am faced with, I still have a greater purpose, and they are tests. Tests that God presents us with reveal our strengths, weaknesses, and truths to which we may not have been privy. It is our task to discover what the journey is while staying motivated and inspired. If you truly desire success and genuinely want it, you will never run out of motivation, inspiration, passion, or energy. It comes from within you! You have to keep your soul nourished so that it can provide you with that internal strength that transcends to the mind. Would you please think of the scenario of a bride-to-be picking out her wedding dress? She may know what kind of dress she wants, but she will say yes to the dress and instantly cry. Imagine you in her shoes and that burst of emotion you would feel.

Now imagine feeling that similar reaction when doing something you love or that can change your life. You need to recognize and accept that we all have a purpose in this world. Unfortunately, if you do not possess that mindset, you cannot pull motivation from no or an undefined drive. Every action has a motive; otherwise, we go through the motions with an almost existential perspective. As we experience different phases in our lifetime, we should find ourselves taking a step back to reevaluate where we are and realign our purpose. This helps us stay connected with ourselves and exercise self-awareness more frequently. I can guarantee you that this will allow you to take a firmer grip on your life and make better decisions when faced with adversity.

Let me ask you some questions, and I want you to sit for a minute and ponder.

What is your definition of success?

Do you feel successful?

Do you feel like you have achieved success in your life?

Once you come up with your answers, try asking people in your life what their definition of success is and if they feel successful. Ask them if they have ever achieved success. Compare your perspective versus theirs, and you will come to realize that success is subjective, and you need to customize your life to accomplish what you deem to be your success. Just because you have your definition of "success" does not mean that that is the same interpretation as someone else.

Yes, we are all people, and we live on the same Earth.

Overall, we all experience similar things in life, but how they happen varies. What are you doing to reach your goal? Do you even have goals that you have set to achieve? Are these attainable goals because goals are different from dreams? These are questions you need to ask yourself to acknowledge your situation. You need to recognize what actions you need to embody to make that change. After you recognize and realize, you need to act. A great way to do this is by displaying your goal and the vision you desire. Close your eyes, breathe deeply and feel the physiological surge of energy that travels through your body. This feeling should be enough motivation to act in making your thoughts turn into reality.

CHAPTER 3

WHAT IS YOUR WHY

In previous chapters, I have mentioned purpose and how to stay motivated to manifest your purpose. Sometimes, it can prove to be a grueling process to get yourself in any momentum. The key to finding your purpose is finding your why. In doing so, you will find yourself becoming less stuck. It is a statement of intent that describes why you wake up every morning and why you do what you do. It distinguishes you from everyone else and is your driving force. It is the purpose, cause, belief, and value that drives you and nourishes your soul. It is a 3-word question that is ideal for those who have reached a level of stagnancy or want a new outlook on how their inner motives, desires, and interests can manifest into something more significant. Understanding it will reveal what motivates you but also leads to a more fulfilling life. A more meaningful life overall.

Once you gain this clarity, you will be able to share it with others. In turn, they will understand you better, giving you the comfort to position yourself around those who share a similar way. When you feel uneasy, dissatisfied, or anxious, it is because you have not found your why. You are living to satisfy someone else's why in the absence of your own. You are not in alignment with your unique purpose. What you are doing now may not align at all with your purpose. Why did you choose what you are doing now? Survival? No choice? Pressure from parents? Did you misjudge your future? These are reasons why you have decided what you do now, but there is no drive coming from within. You have found yourself adapting to the demands of external pressures. Finding your why forces you to look within your inner self and seek what drives you. It will require work and sacrifice, short-term or long-term. Making sacrifices will be easier because the drive that pushes you to pursue will be stronger. It gives you meaning, and it is the true expression of yourself and your identity. It will put you in alignment with your purpose in Life and fuel your work and your lifestyle.

Practicing self-awareness helps you find your why. You can write daily, whether it is in the form of journaling or another method. You can also practice daily self-reflection sessions for an hour or two. We need to bring to light the inner patterns of thinking, reacting, behaving, and habits. If you have found your why, you have put in the necessary work. If you have not, you probably have not been faithful to the process of discovering your genuine why—familiar places to find the motivation to uncover your why are your values, passions, and strengths. Your values set a foundation of what you hold at the utmost. Motivations are the driving forces that keep you interested, the reasons you remind yourself to keep going. Passions are the love for the things you are doing and the need to keep them in your Life. Strengths are tasks or actions that you can do at an excelled level because you have mastered them in a way that allows you to achieve goals.

The best way to learn and implement this practice is through self-experimentation. You know yourself best, so it allows you to challenge yourself to new assumptions and open your mindset to gaining new perspectives on your habits. By asking yourself the following questions, you can begin to unlock your why, the unique driving force that makes you you. You cannot accomplish anything without a clear purpose or goal.

This is the number one director to your success: purposeful meaning.

What is your why?

Why do you wake up every morning and go to work every day?

Why do you wake up and go to school every morning?

Why do you have multiple jobs that you coordinate?

What drives you and helps you feel complete?

Why do you do what you do?

What gives you life?

What brings you joy?

What, if you could have anything, would you choose your life to look like?

What are the little things you find yourself doing everyday that could improve or sabotage your situation?

What do you prioritize and give energy to?

What do you hold close to you when it comes to virtue?

What do you say to yourself during private, intimate conversations with yourself?

CHAPTER 4

"YOU ARE INVINCIBLE" MINDSET

The actual key to success, happiness, abundance, and desires relies upon your mindset. Whether you know it or not, you are invincible, and having this unstoppable mindset is critical to personal development and success. Invincible mindset - what is it exactly? Let us break down the term into separate words for an easier understanding.

Invincible: Possessing an internalized power and being invulnerable to fears and judgment of others. Others cannot easily overcome it.

Mindset: An established set of core values by someone that determines how successful they are.

Now, put them together, and you have what you call the "invincible mindset." The words we use after "I am" determine how we identify ourselves and our place in the world. You can tap into your potential.

The invincible mindset, or IM, represents the most powerful mental tool that a person can possess. You will notice that IM phonetically represents the most powerful words in our vocabulary, "I am." By maintaining an invincible mindset and learning how to master it, you will experience freedom from past limitations and barriers as you learn to focus on the present and let go of the past. This will help you define and mold your reality into the life you have envisioned. What we fail to realize, sometimes, is that as people, we have more in common. Accounting for all of the differences that we may have, we all have something in common no matter who we are. If we are honest and authentic about it, we have all felt moments of inadequacy, anxiety, fear, depression, self-sabotage, and a possible inferiority complex that you are not smart enough, not good enough, not beautiful enough, not light enough. Just…not…enough… This is where moments of self-awareness and implementing the growth mindset are necessary. This gives you the freedom to exercise the invincible mindset and positive I am affirmations that will force you to turn your head away from the past and ahead to the present, which will, in turn, help your future.

Making decisions can happen instantaneously or overnight, but the process that leads you to the destination can not. One day, I told myself that I am invincible and would believe it for one day. No exaggeration whatsoever, I had one of the best days in a long time. The selfaffirmation allowed me to eliminate all fear and doubts about myself, and I noticed an energetic

Sara I had never before experienced. I had control of my thoughts and myself, and I forced myself to think positively. There is nothing wrong with thinking you are invincible, but at the same time, be cautious so as not to be prideful and develop a superiority complex. Humility is everything, and possessing that quality will ultimately get you even further in life than you might think. Contrary to this, however, you can engage in self-sabotage due to your mindset that can lead to actions that will bring you down. It works opposite from the invincible mindset, whereas you should be following I am with positive statements versus negative ones.

I believe we are strong.
I am strong.
You are strong.

I believe you have what it takes to be invincible and possess that mindset. To authentically exude invincible mindset vibes through your actions and decision-making. It is a psychological truth that you are what you think you are, and eventually, thinking will turn into believing. If you think of yourself to be strong, you will believe and be STRONG in the complete sense of the word. If you think you are weak, you will only embody the word and believe you are weak. If you believe you are fragile and will be crushed by circumstances, that is what will happen. Once you choose to let go of this limiting belief and accept a new one - that you can rise above this fragility and pull yourself out of circumstance - you will rise above and be invincible! Finding what having an invincible mindset means for you allows you to function from an unshaken foundation of absolute strength and security.

It is easy to create an invincible mindset but taking on every challenge life throws at you is more intricate! You can still successfully achieve this goal while building resilience and inner strength you never thought you could achieve! So, how exactly do you create an invincible mindset? The cool part about having an invincible mindset and taking on every challenge life throws at you is that it is all about the little things you do. You do not have to make drastic changes in your life for this to become real. Make small changes and do them consistently.

Who you are, or who you think you are, is simply a combination of all your character traits. This can include your personality type, religion, hobbies, profession, strengths and weaknesses, interests, and values. You describe yourself with these character traits combined, but where do they come from? Your habits. What we habitually do becomes part of who we are. We label ourselves based on these things (if I write for a living, I call myself an author; if I like socializing, I call myself an introvert). So, if our character traits come from our habits, where do our patterns come from? When we are in a stressful situation, our brain goes into fight, flight, or freeze mode. The increased chemical reactions in the brain and level of stress may lead us to choose an action that provides near-instant relief and decrease cortisol levels. Because our body chose that action as a form of ease and safety, we can subconsciously continue to react in that same behavior even though that threat is not imposed. We repeat these actions again and again because they are familiar.

But from where do those actions come? **Decisions**. And from where do those decisions come? **Thoughts**.

Stress -- Thoughts -- Decisions -- Actions -- Habits

Thoughts are the root of everything, and we become what we habitually think about. We feel the manifestation of it consuming us; sometimes it can be good, sometimes it can be harmful, even fatal. Stress and any following feelings of anxiety and fear are followed by thoughts, which formulate decisions, make tangible actions, and create habits. This turns into who we are.

It can seem a little daunting to realize that our thoughts do control our entire lives. But who is in actual control of your thoughts? YOU are. At times, it may not feel like it and may feel like your mind has taken over you, and it has a mind of its own. But you do have control and can learn to gain control of your mind. It all starts with choosing to let go and breaking your habits. Exercising a habit-change mindset will free you from feeling stuck and limited due to the limiting mindset. Your mind has habits just like your body does, and you will find yourself using the same thinking patterns repeatedly, even though the situation may not apply anymore. You will try to avoid thinking about something but find yourself absorbed by it. Why? Because your mind is familiar with these thought processes and familiarity provides a safe zone for our body to thrive. Our biology prospers in understanding. On a biological and physiological level, our body does not like change. We get so comfortable with what we have been used to doing for a long time that it almost becomes second nature and does not involve any extra thought. We convince ourselves that things are just fine when in reality, they are not. If you have any negative self-talk floating in your mind (you do, because everyone does), things are not "just fine." You do not want to acquire the average mindset that yields discomfort, dissatisfaction, and unfulfillment. You want an invincible mindset to make your dreams become realistic goals and take on any challenge that comes your way!

The recipe for an invincible mindset is letting go of old beliefs to make room for new ones! You can approach this transformation by creating an attitude of curiosity, kindness, confidence, bravery, and grace. By changing the words in your head, you can transform the way you think. We are our own harshest critics, and most of us criticize ourselves in the cruelest of ways. We think about ourselves negatively, and instead of using good words, we often describe ourselves in reverse. "I am not good enough. I am insecure. I am stupid. I cannot do it." Believe it or not, this is a typical dialogue for the typical person's brain. It is a horrible thing to do and needs to be changed right now. A simple way to transform your brain's dialogue is by engaging in positive self-talk. You can begin your day by looking at your eyes in the mirror and every time a negative "I am" pops in your head, say these four self-loving affirmations instead:

I love you.
I am proud of you.
I believe in you.
I forgive you.
I Love You

Love is the foundation of who you are. We are created to love, from love, and to thrive through the spread of love. If you cannot truly love yourself, how do you expect to love others truly? If you cannot be kind to yourself, how do you expect to extend kindness to others? Love inspires, fills, creates, expands, uplifts, and explodes. Imagine if the joy and love you feel just by being around those you love was how you felt the same way about yourself? How would it make you think to show yourself kindness in your words and your actions? This is what loving yourself means—not calling yourself names that place negative labels on you. You would probably not do that to the person you love, so do not say it to yourself. Love yourself.

I am Proud of You

Pride in oneself is not equivalent to being prideful or arrogant. Arrogance and the ego are, in fact, traits of an insecure person, whereas pride in oneself is a healthier manifestation. When we are in a state of threat or exposure, we tend to lash out with pride. But when we feel proud of ourselves, we experience security, safety, and confidence. Confidence is different from arrogance. I believe confidence comes from character, and conceit comes from ego. Confidence is something that needs to be worked towards and takes time. Confidence is manifested from your deepest thoughts and experiences, and this occurs in our moments of solitude. In our aloneness, we can choose to be confident. You decide to be you, no matter what others may think. There might be a small few people whom we respect enough to care about their opinion, but other than that, you should be free to be you and do you. No one has the permission to make you feel inferior, nor should you give anyone access to that. You are amazing. Be proud of yourself.

I Believe in You

Believing in oneself is not associated with being arrogant, either. It is a matter of how you view and process it. The reality is that in this world, we cannot survive alone. In my previous way of thinking, many of us believe that sometimes it is about doing everything ourselves. You cannot. Instead, you can be the puppet master of your destiny with the choices you make and the belief systems you adopt. God created you with a purpose, and each of us has our unique way of articulating and sharing it with the world. Dreams are different from goals, and both can become a reality. The only person who has what it takes to achieve dreams/goals into reality is YOU. Everything is possible as long as you have the willpower and resilience to get through it. You must have courage and bravery. Close your eyes. Take a deep breath in and out, in and out. Look at your future self and envision what it is that you seek. What it feels like, smells like, looks like, tastes like, and sounds like. Take in, physiologically, how all those senses make you feel, and this is the beginning of the manifestation. Believe in yourself with your whole self.

I Forgive You

Ladies and gentlemen. Let us talk about forgiveness. Forgiveness is probably one of the hardest things one can do to others, let alone oneself. We hold ourselves to the highest criticism and judgment, so of course, it can seem impossible to forgive ourselves. But we must. Not forgiving yourself can cause unbearable physical pain and health issues in areas where you hold in the trauma (in your cells and muscles). What we hold against ourselves is stored away inside, only to eat away at us, making us miserable. I do not believe in regret, but there are certain things we look back on and wish we had not partaken in. We focus too much wasted time on how we fell short and the failures that we do not give ourselves time to process and forgive. Part of learning and becoming a wiser person is making mistakes and learning from them. Actively engaging yourself in understanding how your response or lack of response and how you responded led to the outcome. This allows you to be better prepared if a future similar situation presents itself. You must forgive yourself and let go of all of your failures and mistakes. You are not perfect, nor were you made to be. But you can try to

37

be your best, and that begins by forgiving yourself. Permit yourself to forgive yourself.

You already have the Invincible Mindset within you. Could you find it and fulfill your purpose?

CHAPTER 5

SELF-DISCOVERY

How do you know your purpose? As you are aware, unfortunately, no script or manual tells us how to figure this out. It is a self-discovery process that takes years and even a lifetime to figure out. Self-discovery is a tremendously great thing that demands a lot out of every one of us. It can also be a painful experience but imagine the person you can become at the end of that selfdevelopment. Self-discovery is the foundation on which a solid identity can be built. Since we are forever evolving as people (with the goal and intention of becoming better people), we have to look at the bigger picture; otherwise, it will be an impossible journey. Change is good, but most people do not like or adapt well to change. I have always tried to figure out what it is about me that makes me different from others, and I think I just did! I love the change! Of course, I love and desire stability and consistency; I mean, who does not? Because I can be like a chameleon and adapt to people and situations quickly, I have had a higher success rate when it comes to change in some instances than most people would. I enjoy it and live it. I embody it.

There has to be a medium and a balance between the two, just like everything in life does.

Think about it.

How can you grow as a person, make a difference in your life, and achieve your goals if you are unwilling to allow room for change or growth? Why are you settling for less and not allowing yourself to thrive? That does not make sense and allows for the death of you, not the rebirth. Change is so good and may save a person from following a destructive path. You need to obtain and maintain confidence within you to make the necessary changes you discover in your journey. Personally speaking, my confidence is not heaven-sent by any means. It comes from within me (and with a lot of practice) because I do not care about what people think of me (of course, I care about how God and my mom view me). I spent so much time worrying about what people thought about me that it affected me negatively, and I lost my ability to speak up. Relationships with people are great and can assist in your self-discovery process, but sometimes you have to drop certain ones because they are not helping you grow. Losing a relationship hurts, but losing yourself in a relationship hurts longer and harder. You lose sight of who you are and what your purpose is. Your focus disappears, and you are left feeling lost.

Take control of yourself by gaining the confidence you should have and make the necessary changes to help guide your life in the direction of success. The end of something is always the start of something new.

CHAPTER 6

DOWNFALLS

Each of us has a set of characteristics and traits that make us who we are. Whether they are positive or negative characteristics and qualities, we have a distribution of various mixtures in an individual that make us great. So many great leaders have possessed such exemplary traits, but the one thing in common is the pattern of their downfalls. Their Achilles heel. As we have seen over history, one weakness or lousy way of behavior or thinking caused the end of many civilizations. We have the good and the bad, but I can argue that downfalls are attributed to bad traits that lead to self-sabotage. Unresolved pain and trauma can lead even the most outstanding leader to make tragic mistakes, but it is how we take those mistakes and learn from them.

We each have things we would like to change about ourselves to make us better people inside. We must tap into that openly and without denying ourselves the truth. We have all experienced some level of pain that has made us choose a particular lens through which we view the world. We must let go because it is not healthy. Your pain is only a temporary situation and inconvenience. It will pass. You have to go through to get to your destination because Life is a journey. Downfalls can seem scary, but if you are in a self-reflective mindset, you will have an easier time accepting yourself for who you are and analyzing and implementing changes. Fear of the unknown is an absolute hindrance and a struggle I have always dealt with because I like to control. If I am not, I will not know the outcome, and that scares me. I overcame that when I faced reality because that was a priority to me.

Another major downfall I would like to touch on is the crabs in a bucket mentality. If you have not seen a pot of live crabs, when you do, you will immediately notice that they will climb on top of each other. You would think this would be an instinct to hatch up a plan to get out of the pot. On the contrary, they will climb atop each other to bring each other down. It is a way of thinking that embodies the phrase, "if I cannot have it, neither can you." A syndrome usually comprises a group of similarly situated people who hurt those in their community to get ahead. To elaborate, this applies to people who live in impoverished neighborhoods, and as soon as one receives an opportunity to get ahead, one is faced with jealousy and hate. Instead of supporting the one person to get ahead, they find a way to pull that person down to their level collectively. We need to get out of this toxic way of living as it does no one good. When we physically manifest this kind of mentality, it physically tears down our communities and our potential hope to make it better. People do not want to be left behind but are also not willing to offer anything. It is each of our responsibility not to focus on others but rather ourselves. If we are not where we want to be, do not tear down another. Seek the assistance you need and focus on yourself to learn to live a more colorful life.

CHAPTER 7

FOLLOW-THROUGH

Follow-through is just as important as anything else, and giving up is not an option. I've said it once and I will say it plenty a time. You ultimately fail when you do not try. I know you hear me when I tell you it is easy to say you will start something. As we go through life, certain instances lead us to come up with some great ideas! I have had this occur to me on more than several occasions. But what about the result? Are you one of those people who say they want to do x and get x done, but you either leave it as a thought, or you start and do not finish? I am guilty of the latter more than the former, but I am no better than you. Yes, there are certain things in life that we do not enjoy doing, but sometimes we have no choice but to do them. A general life principle we should commit to is follow-through.

You cannot make a shot in basketball or get a strike in bowling just by throwing the ball. You have got to aim and make sure you follow through with your arm, wrist, and finally your fingers to get a successful shot. When you reduce it to this technique, life works the same way, my friends; Life works the same way. What better feeling than to get something done from start to finish and being able to cross it off your list and say, "Hey, I did that!" It is such an empowering feeling to know you have accomplished something, but that requires followthrough. You have to consider that accountability is crucial for you to meet feasible deadlines in place. My time is golden. I respect my time, so I expect you to respect mine too. You should carry that aura and make it known because life is too short, and we do not have enough time to be wasting. Deadlines are determinants of your success, and they exist for a reason. If you do not have any deadlines, create them to ensure your project gets accomplished accordingly. Please make sure the deadlines are reasonable and feasible so as not to overwhelm yourself and make you give it up completely.

Accountability and follow-through are essential factors that lead to the completion of deadlines, yes. On a larger scale, discipline and consistency are crucial to success. You can do something sporadically and when you feel like it, but the results will not be what you are seeking. If you use discipline and consistency, your outcomes are countless! It will be a pleasant surprise. For example, when I was 21, I decided to run a marathon to commemorate my last year as a University student in Minnesota. To pass the class successfully, we were required to ultimately run the Eau Claire, Wisconsin marathon on May 5th, 2013. I thought it would be a piece of cake. Still, by the end of the experience, I realized that it required a level of discipline, mental preparedness, and consistency in training and pace to prepare and complete it.

We had to train during the winter break, even before the spring semester started. I remember that every Monday, we would have a one-hour lecture at 8 am to learn theory and preparation for this process. Every Wednesday at 8 am, we had a one-hour intensive HIIT training class where they expected us to put in maximum effort. What challenged me the most was that we were required to attend class dressed in our running gear and ready to go at 7 am every Sunday. Whether there was ice, snow, blizzard, or slush, we were expected to show up on time and ready for the run. Sunday was when we would do our long-distance training all around the Twin Cities. The longest distance we ran on a Sunday was 13 miles, and over time, it became easier as my body was able to endure the required stamina. I had the opportunity to experience nature and different parts of the cities, which was a plus. The expectation was for us to train on our own time outside of our scheduled classes, but that was not possible for me. Marathon training was not my only class, and I was just about to graduate! So I had to do what I could, but I will never forget my experience running that marathon on May 5th, 2013.

It was a hot, hot day, and I was able to run the first 13 miles without stopping once. The next 13.2 miles were harrowing as I cried and wanted to give up until I realized that I was stuck in the middle of Eau Claire, Wisconsin. I could only visualize my car and my hotel bed, which gave me the courage to keep going. Six hours, twenty-four minutes, and eleven seconds later, I crossed the finish line and got my medal! I came in 336th out of 340 overall and 156th out of 160 women. Look. I did not run that marathon to compete for time, but I wanted to try something I had never tried before and say, "I did that." Every time I tell this story, I feel so proud of myself for accomplishing that success and deciding to try something new, despite it being challenging and being bedridden for a couple of days. The lessons learned will be remembered and implemented for a lifetime, and with that experience, I proved to myself that

I can do what I set my mind to do.
So can you.

Sometimes, we may not want to do certain things or put ourselves in situations that we usually would not until the circumstance arrives. It would help if you were willing to throw yourself into uncomfortable scenarios threatening your pride and comfort zone. Again, humility is more appealing, so pride should not be there. Put your pride and ego to the side! Successful people did not become so simply by having a chip on their shoulders. Get rid of that vice and humble yourself. You have to start from the bottom, work yourself up, and always remember from where you came. It is easier said than done, but if you want it, you will make it happen.

One thing that I've learned is that people appreciate follow through. What i mean by that is do not be quick to promise something you cannot fulfill. Do not speak in advance about something that is not firmly in place because you are only sabotaging yourself. I've learned that speaking above my turn or too quickly in advance has caused some repercussions.

CHAPTER 8

INTENTION - YOUR HOW

So far, you have a pretty good foundation on the tools for your success. Having intention is powerful, but most people do not recognize that that is the case. In Islam, the intention is everything, and we believe that that can change the outcome of some situations. Are your intentions malicious, or are they geared towards a positive effect? You have the ability to make things happen; your intentions have to be correct. Now that you have your why, we need to work on the how. Once you realize your purpose in life and the reasons that drive your passions (your why), you need the how to make it happen. I have given you that already: set up your intention with the goal of reaching success.

Have the intention to reach your goal by or before your deadline.

Create the intention to help you accomplish your goals and never take "no" for an answer.

Expect to get some rejections, as that is part of the process.

Always have the intention to learn, expand your expertise, educate yourself, and improve.

My mom always taught me that closed mouths do not get fed, and she was right. I had to make it my intention to consciously put in the effort to ask questions in class or speak up in times that I would be afraid to ask for help. I still struggle with that in adulthood, but I am optimistic that one can master a lot with practice and time. You cannot expect people to know what you do or do not want if you do not speak up and verbalize what is on your mind. Communication is critical but effective communication is even more critical when you have a clear intention set.

What is it that you intend to do and accomplish?
What do you intend to communicate?
What is the main point that you would like the other person to understand?

Once you have that figured out, the hows will fall into place for you. Something that works for me is to get rid of negative energy and distractions because they consume my life and direct me away from my priorities. People may be in your life temporarily, but everything always happens for a reason, and you may have met that person to meet someone else someday. It may not be apparent right now, but as long as your intentions are pure, you will be guided to the right path of understanding. Nowadays, it is all about whom you know, not about what you know. You need to intend on accomplishing your goals by yourself without the help of others because if you are the type to depend on others, you are in for a rude awakening.

I have come to learn that in certain circumstances, I must include a mind-frame of, "I have my back, and I am the only one who does. I have my own best interest." You must be careful in life because although you may have the best intentions for yourself and those around you, those people may not have the right intentions concerning you. Everyone is looking for their come-up, and nowadays, the methods used to come up are outrageous! It would help if you created within yourself a level of self-love that is not too over the top but enough to be confident in and happy with yourself. "Selfishness," within moderation, is sometimes okay! Make sure you are living for yourself and not for others. I was doing that for a while and realized I was doing the wrong thing. I came to terms with what I needed to come to terms with, and the weight lifted from my spirit was a beautiful experience. I hope you will realize that living for others is wrong, and you need to immediately shift the focus of the lens to you and your happiness.

Intention is the proper direction to a quality, meaningful life.

CHAPTER 9

———————◆————————

POSITIVE ATTITUDE

If you could change one thing in your life, what would it be? Is there anything in your life that you regret? Take a few moments to answer these questions and think about why you feel that way.

When I come across those questions, my answer is simple. I am not regretful of anything, and I would not change anything because I believe that experiences build and shape you. I am the only person who has my story and combination of experiences that taught me my life lessons. I would be someone else if I had different experiences. I would not be able to write this book with the experiences I have drawn upon if I lived a different life. I am grateful to have had the experiences so far; they have taught me to overcome many barriers, and those accomplishments prepare me for more of what is to come. I know God has a bigger plan for me, and I am excited to see its path.

Had you asked me those questions three years ago, I would have had a completely different answer with a list of complaints to share. But, I have vowed to lead as positive a life as possible, which has changed my perspective on my outlook on life. I have seen significant growth within myself and almost used to doubt reaching this point. I attribute that negative and limited mindset to my choices about those who could enter my circle. I began exerting negative energy on the world, and it did not feel good to me. I have come a long way since the beginning of 2018, and I plan on living my best life in the most humble of ways.

Possessing a positive attitude is everything, and it is a lot easier to smile than frown. If you are negative, you project it! I used to make fun of my sister when she told me that plants respond to positive and negative energy. I told her that was ridiculous and laughed for days, thinking it was a complete joke. Little did I know that I was wrong and responded to this information with a pessimistic outlook. Looking back, I could have absorbed the information and done my research, but instead, I decided to shut the idea down entirely because I did not believe it. But, she was right. I realized that I was executing this type of behavior in all aspects of my life. I came to realize that I might be hindering opportunities because of my negativity.

A positive response from me would have yielded a better conversation and possibly a better outcome to the situation, despite its trivialness. If you are positive, you project it also. Once you recognize that you are negative, the next step is to know what you want in life and cut everything else out. Most importantly, cut off negative energy. It can come in friends, relationships, baggage, stress, environment, living conditions, work, or extracurricular activities. Whatever it is, if it is causing toxicity to your positivity and the good around you, by default, you need to get rid of that as quickly as possible. When it comes to deciding if certain relationships are for you or not, silence is sometimes more powerful than having the last word.

Happiness is a choice that begins with positivity. If you exert positivity, you will receive it back in waves. You have to consciously change your mindset and mentality to accept that you can be successful. What makes a good amount of successful people different from everyone else? They get up tirelessly and work to achieve the greatest in the most humble way. Only you have the actual ability to make the changes you are seeking, and if someone else wants it for you more than you want it for yourself, then your mind is fucked up, and you need a reality check. Change your attitude and perspective towards things, and I promise you, you will have unlocked the door to ample opportunities. Nobody likes negativity other than pessimistic people. Misery loves company. I want to live a happy, joyous life, and I promise you I made that my intention when I decided to write this book, and my life drastically changed.

CHAPTER 10

SECRET STRATEGIES

Earlier in the book, we discussed how important motivation is in jumpstarting your success and making it happen. I am sure you have customized secret strategies that work for you to solidify based on particular circumstances in your life. The most prominent design I use is to always set yourself up for failure. Failure is a given part of any process, but that does not mean you are bad or wrong. It just means you did not approach it the best way at first, and now you can try another avenue. Your destination is the same, but you are driving a car instead of using a plane to get there. Rejection is okay, but a lot of people do not have the mindset to embrace it. Reverse psychology on yourself does not allow for you to be hurt or get distracted by being in your feelings. You have prepared yourself by accepting that you may not get the yes you were looking for, and you have given yourself time to come to terms with it. If you end up getting the yes, imagine how much sweeter it will feel?

I used to work at a scientific staffing agency in Roseville, MN as their Operations Support Manager. One significant life lesson I learned from working there was that for every job opportunity that is out there, there are at least 100-200 other candidates pursuing that same opportunity! So, my advice to you is this. Put in your name and move onto the next, all the while thinking you will not get it because chances are, you will not. But with every no you receive, you are getting closer to the yes you so strongly desire; you have to work hard for it simultaneously. This result has indeed happened to me where I have gotten callbacks for opportunities months later from companies I had no recent memory of applying to. I may not be available to accept those offers at this time, but my point is that when it is your time, it will happen. It will help if you put a lot of faith in the process and yourself. That strategy strongly affects the direction of success in your life.

Other secret strategies that may not be apparent at first glance but work are as follows.

Make sure you know your strengths and weaknesses and what they mean concerning your life.

Rewarding yourself when you have accomplished a goal is a common practice, but it is something many people forget to do. I, for one, am guilty of that! However, do not be absurd and give yourself an outrageous award for hand washing and detailing your car. Yes, you accomplished a huge task because that is not easy to do. However, you know well enough that you do not deserve that iPhone you bought yourself as a reward. Customize the prize to the accomplishment. Not only does it uplift your mood, but it also increases endorphin levels in the brain. It makes you feel good. Little gestures like this to yourself will help motivate you to keep up the hard work and continue on the same path, if not a better one. A surge of endorphins will naturally overtake your dopamine levels.

Endorphins are chemicals that are naturally produced by our nervous system to deal with stress and pain.

Dopamines are essential brain chemicals that influence our mood and feeling of motivation and reward.

Another strategy I love to use is listening to my hype song. It may change depending on the trust, but the message must remain the same. Words are compelling and are the catalyst that fuel action. The songs I choose to motivate me have lyrics that are powerful and have meaning to me. I know you have a piece that gives you the energy to stay focused.

What is it?

You need to do the same and find a song or two or three that inspire and motivate you and listen to the words and message. Feel the connection and let it travel throughout your body, giving you the empowerment you need!

The last strategy that I am completing in my success journey is creating a vision board. As most people are, I am a visual learner, and visualizing things makes you believe that they could be yours. The vision board forces you to specify your dreams, goals, and desires, which help you customize your life to make those visions come to reality. I have learned the intensity of the power of the tongue. Over the last few months, I have verbalized some wants and desires more than ever before, and the outcomes have blown my mind. The power of the tongue and vision boards is so real; I have to warn you to please be careful about what you wish! Vision boards are so helpful, especially for those who have trouble visualizing things, but also for those creative minds like mine that have too many visions and a need to narrow them down. Everybody has it tough, but that is the brainstorming process. No matter how grueling or timeconsuming it may seem, you are working towards something more significant.

Be patient.
Trust the process.
Make your vision board.
Live and speak your dreams into existence.

CHAPTER 11

---◆---

HONOR YOURSELF.

Honor is an important one. You must honor yourself and be kind to yourself. It would be best if you came to a place of understanding your shortcomings while honoring your limits. It is hard work and intimidating to consider. Instead of criticizing and focusing on others, we need to spend that time breaking down our character and ways of thinking. You are not practicing the art of "softening your heart." The reason why we are mean or show hatred towards others is that we dislike or hate ourselves. We feel that about ourselves internally, and we project that to the rest of the world. We must know that it is received precisely in that way. Some personal disconnect or hatred acts as a catalyst for people to act out in distasteful ways. If you find yourself in this predicament, you are not in a state of peace or alignment. This is a problem because how you live your life will be determinant upon your misalignment. Things will likely seem out of control, and unless you tap into the deepest part of your soul, you will struggle to overcome this life adversity.

It is in your human nature to continue in this cycle when the only thing you need to do is be honest with yourself. Simply put, you hate others because you hate yourself. Or, you love others because you love yourself. It is not selfish at all because charity begins at home, and you are your home. So, why cannot you exercise softening your heart towards yourself and see how you effortlessly exude that towards others. Everyone has issues that they must cope with, some worse than others, but nothing we cannot handle. Opening up to yourself, loving yourself, honoring yourself, trusting yourself, being honest with yourself, valuing yourself, and accountability within yourself will help you become more open and welcoming to the change. You don't change or open your heart for anyone but yourself. People tend to fail to realize that it is for their growth and betterment to invest in themselves.

And that is what makes it more challenging.

A common mindset is not willing to do more because change is cumbersome, and the present mind-frame is along the lines of, "Accept me for who I am." That is valid to an extent, but for me, I refuse to accept that excuse. It is easier to force others to accept us as is than to make ourselves change. We feel more in control with the former, but it is the latter that genuinely unlocks what it means to have control and manifest it in a balanced, graceful way.

Coercing others comes from weakness, insecurity, and controlling behavior. Changing oneself and gaining knowledge and wisdom comes from a place of awareness, acceptance, strength, confidence, humility, and stepping back.

We must be cautious of the things we do and say to others. Call it cliche, and I do not mind. I live my life by the motto: treat others how you would like to be treated. I have witnessed how humans are creatures of habit and familiarity. I have learned that we tend to mirror each other when communicating. Knowing this psychological skill, if I give a part of myself to another person, they will more often be inclined to reflect that and reciprocate. If I emanate awkward energy, the other person will mirror that and give off uncomfortable energy, whereas at first, they may not have displayed that behavior. I treat others with kindness, compassion, and lack of judgment (unless they give me a solid reason, not to), and almost one hundred percent of the time, I will get it back, even if it is a delayed response. It will come in the form of cards, gift cards, apologies, and gifts. Unsolicited, of course, but gladly accepted. I know I get it back if I give attitude, so I refrain from that because it will not help me in life. It is a distasteful characteristic.

To change your life, you need to be honest with yourself by honoring yourself. It will allow you to stay in alignment with and be true to yourself. What you do for and to yourself will ultimately be projected to the public. People will perceive you in a certain way, and you want to make sure you are giving off a sense of genuine self in those times. Forget others. You are your first and best advocate. The work begins with you, in you, and for you. Then for others.

By honoring yourself, you hold yourself to your highest standard, and that is nonnegotiable. Imagine the power that instills within you.

CHAPTER 12

———◆———

"YES, AND…" NOT "YES, BUT…" MIND-FRAME

Whether you are familiar with the "Yes, and…" mind-frame or not, the phrase comes from traditional improvisational comedy. It originates from when an improv performer needs to go with the flow of their fellow improv actors' performing choices. They are in a position of working with the given material but adding their own twists. The purpose of this is to connect with the audience directly. I learned this while participating in drama class and the multiple plays I acted in through University.

This type of mindset creativity can be extended to other things if simplified to the basics:
a participant accepts (saying "Yes") another participant's line of thinking and expands on that. How can we apply this to become one of the foundational life skills? By not limiting ourselves to accept either this or that and say, "Yes, and…". What saying "Yes" does is allow you to agree to a specific proposition, consequently creating a sense of cooperation. Saying "No" would

completely shut down the proposal because it ends the only line of communication. In an organizational setting, saying "Yes" opens lines of communication, which encourages people to be more receptive and open-minded to an idea than they may have been. This developmental process makes room for judgment later, so one should practice accepting it instead of immediately judging the idea. By doing so, the conversation is allowed to grow on the idea without objections. The all-encompassing step in this process is by saying "and," which allows for new information. Instead of changing information from the first idea, saying "and" helps build upon it.

Imagine what your world would look like if you could apply this mindset ideation to your own life. Imagine if you began to say, "Yes, and..." for yourself instead of the regular, "Yes, but...". I noticed possessing a "Yes, but..." mindset, which was so limiting to me. My life and trauma coach recently told me that I need to be more compassionate to myself, and through this breakthrough, I have been able to unlock practicing that. Part of that includes saying "Yes, and..." because you allow yourself to be more receptive and open-minded. You open lines of communication with yourself that acknowledge ideas that you usually would not have been open to. The amount of self-empowerment you possess as soon as you say yes and allow more is enough to shift your mindset permanently. Mindset is crucial to almost everything you do. It is vital for growth. No matter how many professional or self-development courses you invest in, you will not receive it if you avoid embracing an open improvement mindset. "Yes, and…" enables that. "Yes, but…" limits that.

You naturally allow yourself to open up to so many more opportunities that you would not embrace due to the old mindset. I want you to shift to a "Yes, and…" approach and naturally think about what is possible for you. I want you to imagine and feel all the ways whatever idea you open up for yourself can give you. Every idea will not be a game-changer.

You can take a vision and bring it to life. All it takes is saying "Yes, and…". See what you can do for yourself.

CHAPTER 13

---◆---

LEARN TO LET GO

I have come to learn that we sometimes hold onto things that may have been of use to us before but are now obsolete. These things can be worldly and nonmaterialistic, but the lesson is that attachment to something is not a healthy manifestation over time. We create objections in times of letting go, leading us to live a life that does not feel free. What are the objections? Objections are the worries that people have about potentially making a change and letting go. It is still a commitment, and they still have to be vulnerable. Letting go allows you to experience things differently than you did before and liberates your soul. Would you not want to undergo personal freedom?

"To let go does not mean to get rid of. To let go means to let be. When we let be with compassion, things come and go on their own." — Jack Kornfield

Letting go has been one of the most recurring themes in my life but one of the hardest to embrace. Holding onto pain does not repair anything. Replaying the past does not change it. Wishing things were different does not make them so. In almost all cases regarding the past, you hold onto something that you hold to be true and then let it go. Letting go is the catalyst for encompassing change. Sometimes, holding onto things is more painful than letting them go, so as impossible as it may seem, you must let go. I have come to learn that by not letting go, you are cheating yourself from creating an authentic sense of self. Holding on to the past will hold you back from knowing who you are and possessing it wholeheartedly. Instead of living a life defined by your history, you should live one characterized by who you want to be.

Trust me; painful feelings can be a source of comfort, especially if you know nothing else. Some people equate the pain and unpleasant emotions of their past to their identity. They have trouble letting go of those feelings because those feelings are their identity. With their pain, they know who they are. Without their pain, they are completely lost, making it impossible for them to let go. When I say "they," I mean "me."

But, I have been able to breakthrough from the main struggles by getting accustomed to the following tips:

I had to understand that the relationships I thought I would have will be different from the ones I have.

It would help if you accepted who you are in this moment and the way other people are, too. It may be hard to accept at first, but you will realize that things do not go as planned. That is okay. Self-awareness will allow your relationships and your part in them to improve. You will also have to accept things about other people. Practicing appreciation, gratitude, and trust in the process will enhance the experience.

When dealing with people, I cannot be invested in the outcome because I have often been disappointed.

I elaborated on this in an earlier chapter, but setting yourself up for disappointment puts you ahead of the mental process. Expectations sometimes keep us stuck because they lead us to fear specific outcomes. There are no guarantees in life, but we expect particular results that have no warranties either. Our needs and expectations will not always be met, and in those times, we must uphold ourselves rationally and appropriately.

This could be seen in the form of setting healthy boundaries or by letting go.

I cannot live in chains when I own the key.

We live with self-limiting beliefs that end up defining who we are. This is not okay! Open up your mind and believe in yourself to accomplish anything you want. If you believe you cannot, you will not. If you believe you can, you will. There will be more people telling you that you cannot. Prove them and yourself wrong.

I cannot control others' actions and thoughts. What I can do is control my actions and thoughts.

This is where people-pleasing comes into play, and I am guilty of that. You cannot change another person, but you can change yourself. Be mindful of the decisions you make and how you choose to show up. Doing everything for everyone will NOT refrain them from being mad at you.

I only need to worry about what I think about myself.

Free yourself from the constraints of other people's judgment. Self-love begins with prioritizing how you feel about yourself and what you do to achieve the highest level of self.

You cannot live by your values if you are living to make others happy.

I must leave room for mistakes because I make plenty of them.

One thing I have had to learn repeatedly is that it is okay to make mistakes and plan for them to occur. Own your mistake and use it as a learning experience. It does not mean you are stupid or incapable; it just proves you are human.

I need to accept the things I cannot change.

This allows you to live in the present moment and not in the "what if" stage. If things were meant to be the way they were, they would. Come to the current as this is where life happens. Yes, past decisions will affect your present and future, but you cannot change the past.

The decisions you make now will open up your future.

I should not be too harsh on myself.

You will be able to experience life's journey in a way that is enjoyable to you. It feels good to laugh with myself and at myself, sometimes, because I am funny. I release tension and enjoy myself for who I am with my presence.

I should do what scares me.

I know, from personal experience, that fear has held me back from doing a lot of things.

It closes our minds to possibilities and experiences that would take us outside our comfort zone.

We should say "Yes, and…" and allow ourselves to experience things outside our comfort zone.

By doing what scares you, you can overcome it and succeed.

I must express openly what aligns and agrees with me.

Instead of bottling up your feelings to please others, express how you feel and make it known that these align with your values. If they work, great. If not, find a respectful and open way to voice it. Expressing your needs is a vital part of feeling good about yourself.

I need to allow myself to feel negative emotions, too.

If you are feeling negative emotions, allow yourself to feel them in whatever way they manifest themselves for you. I know that bottling up your negative emotions makes the recovery process even more painful. Negative feelings are commonly associated with loss, so allow yourself to feel the grief and go through that process. Your healing will be less painful.

I need to learn to forgive.

Forgiveness is the key that unlocks freedom. It is. Resentment and bitterness will lead to an unwillingness to forgive. You are only hurting yourself as you are preventing yourself from growing and living in the present. You are living in the past. Let yourself heal. When you are in a state of forgiveness, you do not forgive the other person. You forgive yourself by letting go.

You are not what has happened to you.
You are what you choose to become.
Letting go requires gaining a solid sense of self, which you can achieve. Just believe.

CHAPTER 14:

LEARN TO WORK WITH NOT AGAINST OTHERS

In my intro chapter, I remember telling you that I have a large binder of all my educational accolades and certifications down to videos and recordings of celebrations, ceremonies and copious photo albums, full of pictures that my parents took over the years. My parents did not have the best chance at education, so they learned from their experiences and pushed my siblings and I to really excel in school and have a solid educational foundation before pursuing anything else in life. Something that was and is still instilled in me is not only graduating high school, but also graduating with as high of a distinction as possible.

Looking back, I know the kind of efforts that I had to put in to get a satisfactory report card at the end of each year. Even progress reports had to be on par with those expectations at home. My parents never let us slack off, and if we did there were consequences. My parents each handled the consequences differently, however, the point is that there were consequences if I did not excel in school. My parents were loving, but strict when it came to education, and there was no joke because they understood the struggles of not having a solid educational foundation.

As such, my parents decided to enroll me into an American international school in

Riyadh, Saudi Arabia, which is an American accredited international school for Expat children. We were given the privilege of being students there from pre-K up until my senior year in high school, even though that is not where I graduated from, ultimately.

Looking at my life as a linear timeline, I can see the multiple spots or multiple lines on that master timeline, where I have had to work with, and interact with groups of people, if not another person. Yes, I did grow up in a very sheltered and protected way, but at the same time I still had a certain idea that working with others is important and unavoidable in life. I remember back in my middle school, high school, and university days, when our teacher would have us do group projects. I remember having a dreaded feeling encompassing my soul.

Why did I have a dreaded feeling overcoming me in those moments? Because I knew the kind of work ethic that I had and I was a very strong perfectionist at the time. I was very anxious, which I would control with my OCD-like behaviors and try to control situations and other people. I did not realize I was engaging in these types of behaviors as that was something that was normal to me, and not a dysfunctional behavior. Those were the scope of my skills at the time. However, I accepted the fact that I would have to work with this team to achieve a common goal and get a good grade. I always try to have a positive attitude and positive mindset when approaching the situation. My hesitation lied in the common outcome that I would be the one who would put the most work and effort in the project.

As such, I was not very enthusiastic for the next opportunity to engage in teamwork again. I personally knew the level of teamwork I was willing to and would end up giving, but the funny part is my classmates knew and unexpected that of me as well. So when they ended up being my partner they were super excited because they knew that they would succeed and ace the project, and 100% of the time that's what the outcome was. I did not feel 100% okay with this, and obviously I felt disturbed by it each time it happened, and that is why I did not necessarily enjoy having to work in teams. I was content working by myself and putting in whatever was necessary to achieve the goal.

I am self learned in so many different types of fields, as a result of these past experiences. I wanted to start to experience something new. I have learned over the years, after becoming a coach, and having had different difficult experiences to grow from, that it is highly crucial to a better and positive interaction to have clear communication, to set clear boundaries, and to make sure that I am clearly communicating with the other person or other team members. What are the expectations? What are the outcomes and how can we achieve this realistically? In the past, I did not have the skills to be able to express myself alongside working in a team. But now, I have learned that teamwork makes the dream work, but there have to be specific teammates who understand the task at hand and have a similar goal as you in order to reach that outcome.

I have worked and left so many jobs because of the lack of compatibility with the team members. Now, I am not perfect, however, I have made a conscious effort to grow, change myself, and learn, so as to experience a better life. What you put out there is what you attract, so if I can put out a healthy form of communication and teamwork, I am hoping that that will reflect to the recipients where they can give that back to me. By not learning how to work with other people, you will find that you are hindering your personal growth and abilities to see the beauty of what others have to offer.

I have learned to ask for help because I realize I cannot do everything by myself. That is why there are so many specialties, fields, niches, and people with talents and skills of various kinds. We are here to be resources for each other and need to learn how to ask for those resources, but not take advantage of them at the same time. Giving ourselves to help others and to ask for help only serves to benefit us at the end of the day. We can learn skills, tools, knowledge, ability, and wisdom from others through teamwork and open and direct communication. Yes, we may have triggers and frustrations, but the more we learn and accept to work with other people, the more we gain the resilience to interact and work with them. It becomes easier and more fun to interact with others when you can learn to be on the same page. Resilience is a major factor in this. Take each experience as a way to grow and improve your communication and teamwork skills so hopefully your actions will speak louder than your words to teach others to do the same.

There is an African proverb that says "If you want to go fast, go alone. If you want to go far, go together." Going fast was such a priority to me, that I lost sight of the value of teamwork. As soon as I started to embrace the idea of working with others and learning from it, so many opportunities started to abundantly fall into my lap. I have become so acclimated to working with others and asking for help, that that human interaction is something I yearn for and I am not afraid to ask for assistance or ask for others to give me their feedback. We are our worst critics, so sometimes we are over analyzing something that another might not even have noticed. I feel that it is important to learn to work with others and the value of teamwork is something that we need to be taught in school on a less superficial level.

CHAPTER 15

---◆---

SELF-CARE

Change and transformation can be and feel daunting, especially if we do not know what to expect. We can prepare ourselves as much as we possibly can as far as expectations go, but we have to accept the fact that we may not know 100% of what to expect at the beginning of our journey. Transformation and change have a lot of unknown areas, which I previously mentioned as the gray area, so self-love is something that is crucial, and plays a major role in this story.

To me, self-love and self-care are synonymous. What this looks like for me, is anything to do with nourishing my soul and preparing me for aligning my inner and outer peace. Self-love and self-care include the word self because it is all about you. This is the one time where being selfish has nothing to do with giving yourself the love and care you need. The only way to be able to show up for others and primarily yourself, is by filling up your cup first. If you have flown in a plane, you will remember that at an emergency landing, you are required to put your oxygen mask on first before you put it on others. So, self-care and love are the foundational steps towards a healthy start to healing.

During self-love, we need to learn to fall in love with ourselves. We need to use this time to do anything that we need to take care of ourselves so we can stay physically, mentally, and emotionally full. There are seven types of self-care that range in the categories of mental, emotional, physical, environmental, spiritual, recreational, and social. How we do one thing is how we do everything, so a well-balanced self-care routine involves each of these. Make sure that you avoid restricting yourself to just one or two of these types of self-care, because in order to be whole, we need to address them all.

By focusing on our self-care, we can amplify our ability to stay physically, mentally, and emotionally strong and stable. It will allow us to show up in the best way possible, and in more alignment with how we want to show up. I have a vivid memory of when I was having a therapy session and my therapist asked me what I do for self-care. I was speechless, because I had no idea what self-care and self-love even meant. I got very emotional and started to cry, because I realized how much I was neglecting myself, and how harsh I had been on myself. Thus far, this was a huge wake up call for me, and my homework after that session was for me to process ways in which I could engage in self-care. The example that my therapist gave me, and I will never forget this, because of the simplicity of it, but the benefit of it as well, was to lotion my body from head to toe after each shower. The purpose of this action is to take a moment to love and appreciate my body and skin by rubbing love and attention all over it. A lot of other things came into perspective for me at that moment.

Some of the ways in which I decided to change myself and start incorporating self care was by starting to maintain a regular sleeping routine, eating healthier and working out more, spending more time outdoors and in nature, identifying the things that I like to do but don't do as a result of not wanting to do them alone, doing hobbies that I enjoy, but most importantly, focusing on expressing gratitude. Gratitude is so pivotal in appreciating what you have in life and seeing things for what they really are instead of through the lens of what you want.

Gratitude is the golden key to healing and abundance. If you can incorporate this in your self-care practices and focus on positivity and staying connected with what is true to you and what will revitalize you from inside out, that is what you need to focus on. What are ways in which you engage in self-care to improve your life and show up better?

CHAPTER 16

FINAL MESSAGE

We have reached the end of this particular encounter to motivate you in your life and reach whatever successes you have planned for yourself. It takes a lot and is a lifestyle change that does not come easily to most. Positivity and happiness are choices you have to make that will eventually become a lifestyle. Be smart about your decisions and how you approach life. Be meaningful in your actions and words but most importantly, be genuine because it is true that the world gives you back the same energy you give it. You need to remember God if that is your belief and wholeheartedly ask for His guidance and prosperity. You need to acknowledge, recognize, and react in a way that will make your epiphany a reality. It would be best if you discovered your purpose and the reason as to why you get through every single day to get through tomorrow. It would help if you had the mindset that you are invincible, but humility is critical. You must be open to the process of self-discovery and change, which will lead you to better handle any downfalls due to outside forces or even your excuses. You cannot make a successful shot without follow-through and a clear intention as to how you will reach your goals. You must always maintain a positive attitude and look at the bright side of every situation, and you will be able to live a happier, more fulfilling life. Only you know what strategies you can implement that work best for you and your lifestyle, so make sure you clearly understand your strengths and weaknesses and how you can use them to your advantage.

We only have one life to live, so please make the most of it. Know precisely what you want in life and accept nothing less, and do not stress over anything that is not helping you improve your life. You may or may not agree with the things I have shared, but I am speaking from experience and observation. Strategies that have worked for me may not necessarily work for you, but I hope you have learned at least one thing that you will implement in your life and see the fruits of your efforts! I give that tough love, but I know what to say because I speak from my personal experiences, and that is why I can confidently push people and provide them with advice because I have been there and done that. I want to leave you with this quote I came across, by Buddha, scribbled in my notes: "What you think, you become. What you feel, you attract. What you imagine, you create. With our imagination, the possibilities of creation are endless."

I will not stop until I live my best life, and I hope I have given you the necessary tools to start living your best life!

ABOUT THE AUTHOR

Sara **Nur** is the founder, president, and CEO of Revitalized Living, LLC, a company that helps provide clients who are ready for transformation with systems, support, and accountability, all through purposeful individual and group coaching programs. Sara's coaching style is client-centered and her services focus on transforming your life through the power of habit change. Her specialty is in abundance and transformational coaching. With Sara's eccentric energy, positivity, faith, coaching style, inclusion, openness, and wisdom, revitalize your life and attract the most abundant and healed version of you.

Individualizing her relationships allows her to support people and her clients in harnessing the power of mind, body, and spirit. She has witnessed clients experience deep healing and transformational life changes, beginning with herself and her story. In the midst of her own health and life crises, Sara became determined to heal as naturally and safely as possible from several life and health conditions that had previously left her feeling less than whole. When she was finally ready to seek the help she knew she needed, her search continued endlessly. Ultimately, Sara became the coach that she needed during her transformation, but could not find. That is what makes her unique.

Sara highly values integrity, principle, diversity, equity and inclusion, and strong communication skills. She is a divergent thinker and can use her skills laterally with no limits. Her open-minded disposition allows her to solve problems realistically and reasonably, and with compassion and empathy. She has been renamed as "Sunshine Sara" by a few due to the passion, enthusiasm, vibrancy, energy, and light she brings to every interaction. She has learned to meet people where they are and help them grow based on their personal needs, not her own. Putting others first brings her joy and fulfillment. She uses these skills comprehensively to exude the best version of herself to inspire and lead others to do the same for themselves. As a leader, Sara has the courage and strength to inspire others to discover their self-motivation.

Sara is a quadruple-certified transformational health and life coach (certified through Health Coach Institute) and has extensive NLP training. She has spent the last 15 years as a health advocate (dental, medical, lab, group homes) and decided to merge the fields with coaching. With her passion, Sara guides clients to revitalized living and fullness, to release their inner power and voice. She creates a safe space for individuals to honor their needs, own their power, and speak their truth. It is a 100% no-judgment zone.

Growing up as a third-culture-kid with a Saudi Arabian, Eritrean and Ethiopian heritage, Sara's life pursuits have been multidisciplinary, including her Bachelor of Arts degree in Biology, Society, and Environment, received from the University of Minnesota. Some of her other achievements include being featured in VoyageATL Magazine in August 2022 as a small business, and serving as a coach partner at Kossie. She plans on publishing more books and providing more knowledge and resources to empower others.

You can find Sara on Facebook at:

http://facebook.com/coachsaranur; on Instagram at: @saracoaches and @sarz.world; on Kossie at: https://kossie.co.uk/link/saranur; at her website: https://revitalizedliving.me; via email at:

sara@revitalizedliving.me; and by phone at:
(404) 666-8857.

SUCCESS STORIES

I've had the honor and privilege of coaching Sara Nur for a year, and I'm in awe of her brilliance and authenticity. It takes courage to pivot an already successful life and career into a new direction. Sara's courage is backed by faith and tenacity because she believes in her vision and won't give up. She's open to feedback and growth and brings passion to whatever she's doing. I'm so blessed to know Sara and I know she's here to share her many gifts with those lucky enough to be coached and supported by her.

-Coach Kari Morin

WOW I'm impressed. Sara's coaching and guidance was way better than I expected and much more helpful. I didn't know much about 'personal boundaries' until Sara gave this guidance to me. :) Thank youuu.

-Anonymous

Sara is the perfect example of being both a friend and coach at the same time. She is very welcoming and easy to talk to and relate, making it safe and easy to open up and talk about the   hard stuff we are battling with. Her passions and focus for equity, diversity, and inclusion in society, family, and in the workforce has built a sense of foundation and grounding to stand on your own two feet, proclaiming your values and identity, while still being able to coexist in this universe, while also healing from the hurt of discrimination.

-Coach Mason Van Katwyk

Thank you for giving me emotional support and useful guidelines! I will grab my notebook and answer your questions. :)

-Anonymous

Getting coached by Sara helped plant seeds that have encouraged me to make some major life changes over the past year. I learned about how certain foods cause inflammation and bloating, and how simple things such as how you're eating your food and the span of times in which you eat can help increase your metabolism and aid in weight loss. Speaking with Sara on a weekly basis, about learning new habits and identifying delayed gratification, was helpful with being more intentional, aware, and mindful of my day to day. Working with Sara has overall enhanced my health and other life areas. Thank you, Sara!!

-Yasmine N.

Sara always knows what to say and how to say it. She always has the best insights, it's crazy. Sara has a strategic, organized mindset that allows her to excel as a powerful coach. Her strong sense of intuition and compassion have provided the safest space I have been in for this kind of work. I cannot emphasize enough how invaluable SARA IS!

-Lolla N.

It was a true pleasure working with Sara. I was able to uncover what has been holding me back and confidently break down habits I didn't know I had created in the past. Sara helped me change my debilitating habits without me even having to remember I was being different! I have never experienced anything like it before! Amazing experience so far.

-Hanoke A.

I love your energy and ability to engage. I know you're going to transform many lives with your blessing. You have a character that is timeless in virtue and impeccable even in disguise.

-Simon G.

You were amazing during your workshop today! Your passion shines through every ounce of your being. You are on the right path.

-Jenn H.

It was an honor to work with you! You have the many gifts including youth and time.

God can do so much with a person like you.

-Dr. Bart P.

You have helped me with my transformation. Your voice is what got me out of bed in the morning to work out – now it's become a habit I love to do!1 Also, I am super motivated to declutter, organize, and set boundaries. This coming week will be a productive one. I can feel it, thanks to you! Also… meant to tell you. Impressive you looked up coaching questions on procrastination. They were excellent! But the fact that you went the extra mile shows what kind of coach you are; a big hearted sensitive one to your client's needs. Thank you! Can't wait for our next session and yes, YOU helped me break through the biggest challenge I had in my life to motivate myself to establish a morning routine. Keeping an open mind and testing out new material is what makes you an exceptional coach.

-Alessandra E.

INTERVIEW WITH SARA

HOW LONG HAVE YOU BEEN DOING WHAT YOU DO AND HOW DID YOU GET TO BE A HEALTH AND LIFE COACH?

In some ways, my whole life I've been preparing to become a coach, and I see that now. I was born and raised in Saudi Arabia, also lived in the UK for a time, and have been living and working in the US for 15 years. I like to call myself a Third Culture Kid! I've worked in the healthcare industry for a decade and a half in various roles, and I've experienced and observed so many settings where people interact and communicate their needs, show up vulnerable, feel seen and heard and served, or not. My attention has always been on how people treat each other and how individuals advocate for the support they need in order to feel and be their best selves!

I first learned about coaching when I was living in Atlanta, Georgia back in 2018, and I actually went home to Minnesota to visit my family that October. What's interesting is that I had no idea I had the abilities or skills to coach someone or be able to give that direct, "tough love" that someone needs, but knows that it's coming from a loving place. So I unknowingly coached my big sister Lolla to navigate through a personal situation that was occurring at the time. And I really did not believe in myself. I told myself the roles have been reversed and big sis is actually asking for my help. So it was really great to be given an opportunity to show my skills, my assertiveness, my leadership abilities, and my firmness to help her navigate through a personal situation.

We were able to successfully achieve a positive and reasonable outcome based on my coaching abilities and it was a very empowering experience because at that time, little did anyone know that I had been eight months into working at a hospital. I decided to take my mom's advice and had transitioned roles earlier that year from dentistry into medicine. Little did I know about the underlying politics and policies of hospitals that don't necessarily bring out the best in people. I was at a point in my life where the healthcare industry was extremely overwhelming for me and somehow brought out my people-pleasing weaknesses. My anxiety was amplified and I was very unhappy.

I was having panic attacks at my cubicle, silently vomiting in my trash, and crying endless tears I couldn't control. I felt completely misaligned in all of the five areas of life.

In that moment, my soul and inner-child cried out, *"There's got to be more for me than this."* Through EAP services, I located a therapist who was as closely aligned with my values, beliefs, and struggles. She helped me learn very basic, but useful skills that would be hard for me to resist. She kept it real and that's exactly what I needed because I didn't know what was real anymore.

What seemed like a series of unfortunate events became a series of fortunate ones, once I was able to approach the situation with a grateful mindset. When my sister was able to achieve her goal through my coaching, her push opened the door for me to consider becoming a coach. That night was the night I decided to do some research. I was skeptical at first, and it took me almost six more months of marinating and procrastinating, until I made the life-changing decision to enroll in my first coaching program. Since then, I have achieved four certifications. I began in October 2018 and I ended in October of 2022. Full circle. Ever since then, my life has transformed drastically. And I never looked back. Knowing what I know now, I wouldn't trade it for anything.

WHAT KINDS OF CLIENTS DO YOU WORK WITH?

I am a physical bridge and catalyst for change, especially when it comes to diversity and inclusion. I work with individuals and organizations who struggle with understanding what abundance and healing looks like, and how vital it is to the health of any company or organization. They are ready for the creation of pipelines and a step-by-step system to end the pain of feeling stuck and not getting to experience a healed and abundant life. They are ready to let go of habits that once served a purpose, but are now creating sabotage. They are ready to learn and receive so they can experience cultural inclusion, diversity of thought, and the richness of what life has to offer.

My programs are designed to bring you **culture, healing, innovation, transformation, and abundance** through a **client-centered** focus. I am a sedulous person, meaning, I work hard and don't give up easily. That is the kind of client I am looking for; a sedulous one. Transformation is not easy, but it damn sure is possible.

HOW ARE YOU DIFFERENT FROM OTHER HEALTH AND LIFE COACHES?

———◆———

Most coaches give you a checklist of things to change and do. My work goes deeper, for a couple of reasons. First, I'm not here to give advice, that's not what coaches are for. I partner with my clients to first identify their goals, dreams, and to bring to the surface their gifts and strengths. Then, our focus becomes solving and reframing the real and perceived obstacles keeping them stuck, feeling alone, and non-abundant.

So "Do this, not that" doesn't work because feeling stuck is not about shortcuts or instant gratification, it's about our inability to face reality and get out of complacency. It's about us not wanting to make changes that will trigger our fight/flight/freeze response. Keeping everything the same may no longer serve us the purpose it once did.

So, first and foremost, my **client-centered coaching** is about transforming beliefs and mindsets so that my clients can be present with themselves and their lives in a whole new way. I follow that work with step-by-step guidelines around healthy ways to approach abundance and healing in the form of diversity, equity, and inclusion. I have completed mastery level training in the Transformational Coaching Method (certification program based in Neuro Linguistic Programming), which uses perceptual, behavioral, and communication techniques to make it easier for people to change their thoughts and actions.

I help you take perceptual positions, which is taking another position outside of the view that you may normally hold (you; the other person's view; as an observer or fly on the wall; that which is greater – the most expansive perspective we can access; and as the coach).

Something else that makes me different from other life coaches is that I ONLY work with those who are ready to experience the endless possibilities and abundance that healing can bring. I help individuals and organizations create new systems to replace their obsolete ones that no longer provide a service. In other words, I am not a Jill-of-all-trades life coach. I happily refer clients who aren't a fit for my niche to other coaches I know and trust.

What that means for you is that I am very focused on anything and everything that works for my client who wants to experience the gift of abundance through healing.

Because my focus is very narrow and I have personal experience overcoming these challenges, what you get with me is a deep level of expertise on what works to recover from non-abundance. I bring **innovation, transformation, and empowerment**. I've become an expert at this topic and that's why my clients get great results that they are thrilled with – and we have a lot of fun along the way!

WHAT TYPE OF PERSONALITIES DO YOU WORK BEST WITH AND WHAT IS EXPECTED OF ME?

My Total Empowerment Transformation programs were created for individuals who are absolutely ready and fully committed to having a new relationship to healing and abundance, to ending the fear of accepting change, and compulsively making unreasonable decisions for shortterm gains.

These programs were created for you to put systems around abundance and healing in place in
30, 60, and 90 days, which will eventually lead you to having an experience of peace and even JOY in your life and with transformation.

Consider what you'll do with me to be a transformational experience where you're consistently taking action. No more worrying that you'll never find something that works for you; you'll open up to a very different way of thinking and full support while you achieve this incredibly exciting goal: ending war with the same-old-same and banal so you can experience a Total Empowerment Transformation.

WHO DOES THIS PROGRAM NOT WORK FOR?

———————————◆———————————

I only have openings for 2-3 new clients per month in my schedule, so please know I'm very selective about who I work with, choosing to (gently) turn away people who aren't suited for my program and won't get the results they would have invested in. (It wouldn't be fair to them.)

The Total Empowerment Transformation is NOT for those who aren't ready to commit to and invest the time in their growth and transformation. It is also NOT for those who just want a checklist of things to accomplish and mark off or "do this, not that" (because if that worked for my type of client, it would have worked already).

WHAT EXACTLY IS YOUR SYSTEM AND WHAT DOES IT INCLUDE?
The Total Empowerment Transformation system is a holistic journey that involves mind, body, and soul healing.

We're going to cover all things abundance and healing using the "6W Questions" - remember those from 6th grade when you learned about journalism or critical thinking?

The "6W Questions" are:

What	When	How
Where	Why	Who

The "6W Questions" constitute a simple formula for getting the complete story on any subject.

When I'm working with you as my client, we are definitely looking for the COMPLETE story around abundance and healing.

That's why, in Total Empowerment Transformation, I'll walk you step-by-step through...

What to heal/add abundance to	*When* to heal/add abundance
How to heal/add abundance	*Where* to heal/add abundance

And most importantly...

Why YOU heal/have abundance	Who YOU are being when YOU heal/have abundance

Chances are good that other "methods" haven't worked in the past because they didn't have the steps that addressed every part of you - mind, body, and soul.

Total Empowerment Transformation solves that problem.

In addition to these steps, you will learn tons of tips, tricks, and strategies to manage your health and your life more easily and to make your health and your life work for YOU (instead of the other way around).

DOES THIS REALLY WORK?

Yes! The result of our work is an approach to abundance and healing that has you feeling peaceful, powerful, and on purpose, maybe for the first time in your life.

Be sure to read the Success Stories chapter in this book to read the stories of individuals just like you who have gotten this kind of result.

WHAT EXACTLY IS YOUR SYSTEM AND WHAT DOES IT INCLUDE?

You can expect to:

- the four areas of healing (physical, emotional, spiritual, social Create a vision for what your Total Empowerment Transformation looks like
- Anchor into your Big Why (this is the real reason why making this change matters!)
- Clear clutter (emotional and physical) from your life so you can make space for the new you

- Get specifics on how to approach healing by:
○ Understanding)
   ○ Upgrading the quality of healing you are implement
○ Uncovering your secret weapon around healing, which is HOW you're implementing your healing

   ○ Incorporating an abundant mindset
   ○ Phasing in things and people that give you healing
   ○ Phasing out things and people that take away from your healing
   ○ Learning the forms in which abundance presents itself
○ Uncovering the "inner," "inter," and "external" relationships to healing and abundance

- Optimize your lifestyle by:
○ Discovering all the nutrients that we don't always make room for, but feed your body and your soul, like:

   - Sleep & Movement
   - Love & Sex
   - Fun & Play

- Connection to God, He who is Greater
  - Being honest about what's working and what's not working in your career, relationships, family life, spiritual connection, and more (where do you say "yes" when you really mean "no"?)
  - Learning how to receive help and support (you're always giving, but who's giving back to you?)
  - Put yourself and your health first (this is YOUR time - no more putting yourself last on the priority list)

HOW QUICKLY CAN I EXPECT TO GET RESULTS?

Your transformation begins the second you say "YES" and continues every day throughout your 90-day experience and beyond.

HOW CAN I GUARANTEE MYSELF THAT I WILL ACHIEVE A MORE EMPOWERED, HEALED, AND ABUNDANT STANCE IN MY PERSONAL AND PROFESSIONAL LIFE?

If you've tried things and failed in the past, chances are good that you didn't have the right support, the right system, or the right accountability.

In the Total Empowerment Transformation, you'll get all of these.

Part of the reason for the significant investment in this experience is to ensure that you show up for yourself like never before.

WILL I RECOVER THE INVESTMENT I PUT INTO THIS COACHING PROGRAM?

If you add up everything you've spent over the years on courses and vacations and all the ways you've lost opportunities due to lack of an abundant and healed mindset, how much would that be? How much have you already lost due to your non-inclusive behaviors and ways of thinking to the point that YOUR life is no longer enriched?

If things don't change, how much would you spend in the coming years searching for a solution?

For most of my clients, the answer to all questions is A LOT.

I want you to stop reading for just one moment to ask yourself, "What is a new relationship to people, thought, culture, and other forms of abundance worth to me?"

The information and skills you learn – and the personal transformation you make – with the Total Empowerment Transformation will be with you forever, transforming your quality of life, thought, and health in so many ways.

Sara, based on everything I've read and heard about you, I know you're the one I want to learn from. How do I get started?

Congratulations on making a decision for transforming and empowering your life!
I'm honored and excited to be your guide on this journey!

Here's how we get started:
- During our initial conversation, you can officially enroll in the Total Empowerment Transformation.
- I'll walk you through how to make the investment (I accept all major credit cards, so processing the investment will be easy).
- We'll choose a recurring day of the week and time for your sessions.
  o These sessions should be considered a sacred time – they are first priority because YOU are first priority.
  o Sessions will occur once per week for 90 days.
- I'll send you a "Welcome Email" that includes a **Coaching Program Agreement** (you'll sign this agreement before our first session)

Do people ever renew and continue working with you?

Yes, many of my clients want to continue the work – they love the on-going support and stretch. If that's something you'd like, I'll share how you can do that as we get closer to the completion of your first TET experience.

OK, I'm ready to do this for myself, but I have a couple of additional questions. Can we address them in our Breakthrough Session?

Absolutely. We'll be sure to cover all of your questions, plus the Breakthrough Session will give you firsthand experience of what it would feel to have a powerful coach and mentor in your corner.

Made in the USA
Columbia, SC
06 September 2023